The Beginner's Guide to DRAWING

Written and illustrated by Amy Bailey Muehlenhardt

ANIMALS, BUGS, DINOSAURS, and other cool stuff!!

Capstone press

Table of Contents

Chapter Three: Dinosaurs

Chapter Four: Cool Stuff

Everyone Is an Artist
There is no right or wrong way to draw!

With a little patience and some practice, anyone can learn to draw. Did you know every picture begins as a simple shape? If you can draw shapes, you can draw anything.

The Basics of Drawing

line—a long mark made by a pen, a pencil, or another tool

guideline—a line used to help you draw; the guideline will be erased when your drawing is almost complete

shade—to color in with your pencil

value—the lightness or darkness of an object

shape—the form or outline of an object or figure

diagonal—a shape or line that leans to the side

Before you begin, you will need

- a pencil
- an eraser
- lots of paper!

Four Tips for Drawing

1. Draw very lightly.
Try drawing light, medium, and dark lines. The softer you press, the lighter the lines will be.

2. Draw your shapes.
When you are finished drawing, connect your shapes with a sketch line.

3. Add details.
Details are small things that make a good picture even better.

4. Color your art.
Use your colored pencils, crayons, or markers to create backgrounds.

Let's get started!

Simple shapes help you draw.

Practice drawing these shapes before you begin:

 **circle**
A circle is round like a bouncing ball.

 **triangle**
A triangle has three sides and three corners.

 **oval**
An oval is a circle with its cheeks sucked in.

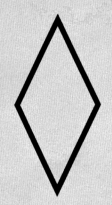 **diamond**
A diamond is two triangles put together.

 **arc**
An arc is half of a circle. It looks like a turtle's shell.

 **square**
A square has four equal sides and four corners.

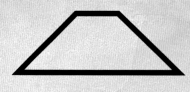 **trapezoid**
A trapezoid has four sides and four corners. Two of its sides are different lengths.

 **crescent**
A crescent looks like a banana.

 **rectangle**
A rectangle has two long sides, two short sides, and four corners.

You will also use lines when drawing.

Practice drawing these lines:

vertical
A vertical line stands tall like a tree.

horizontal
A horizontal line lies down and takes a nap.

diagonal
A diagonal line leans to the side.

dizzy
A dizzy line spins around and around.

zigzag
A zigzag line is sharp and pointy.

wavy
A wavy line moves up and down like a roller coaster.

Remember to practice drawing.

While using this book, you may want to stop drawing at step five or six. That's great! Everyone is at a different drawing level.

Don't worry if your picture isn't perfect. The important thing is to have fun. You may wish to add details to your drawing. Is your dog on a leash? Is he chewing on a bone?

Be creative!

Chapter One

ANIMALS

Basset Hound

The basset hound is a medium-sized hunting dog. The hound has a keen nose for smelling things far away. Hounds have thick coats. They are great family dogs.

Step 1
Draw an oval for the head. Draw a smaller oval for the snout. This oval should overlap the first oval. Add two long ovals for the ears.

Step 2
Add a circle for the chest and an oval for the body.

Step 3
Add two squares for the short front legs. Draw two ovals for the front paws.

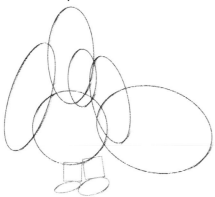

Step 4
Draw a circle and an oval for a back leg. Add a crescent tail.

Step 5

Draw arcs for the eyes and a triangle for the nose. Connect the shapes with a darker, sketchy line.

Step 6

Using the side of your pencil, begin shading. Erase the lines you no longer need.

Step 7

Continue shading. Basset hounds have wavy lines under their eyes. Smudge the lines with your finger.

Bulldog

The bulldog came from England. It is a very courageous dog. A bulldog has a short and powerful jaw. The bulldog is known for being gentle and affectionate.

Step 1

Draw a rectangle for the body. Draw a circle for the head.

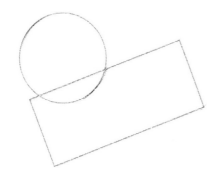

Step 2

Draw a smaller circle for the snout. Add two triangle ears.

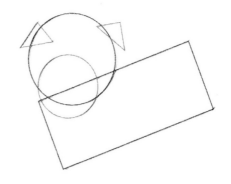

Step 3

Draw four rectangles for the legs and four squares for the feet.

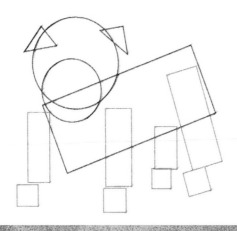

Step 4

Draw two arcs for the eyes. Add a triangle for the nose. Draw two crescents for the mouth and tail.

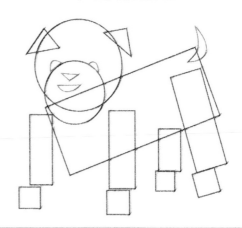

Step 5

Connect the shapes with a darker, sketchy line. Add curved lines for the sagging cheeks.

Step 6

Using the side of your pencil, begin shading. Erase the lines you no longer need.

Step 7

Continue shading. Make the eyes, nose, and mouth darker than the rest of the face.

Golden Retriever

Golden retrievers are powerful and active. They are very friendly toward people and even other dogs. Golden retrievers are very intelligent. They love to run and play.

Step 1

Draw two circles for the head and snout. Add two ovals for ears.

Step 2

Draw an oval for the lower jaw. The oval should overlap the circle.

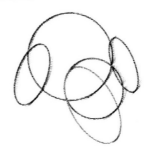

Step 3

Draw an oval for the tongue and an oval for the upper part of the body.

Step 4

Draw two ovals for eyes and an oval for the nose.

Step 5
Connect your shapes with a darker, sketchy line. Draw the nostrils with curved lines.

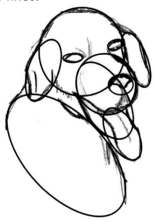

Step 6
Begin adding short, wavy lines for fur. Erase the lines you no longer need.

Step 7
Shade in with your pencil. Make the eyes, nose, and mouth darker than the rest of the face.

Airedale Terrier

Airedale terriers have short, wiry coats. They were first used for hunting in England. The Airedale is known as the king of all sporting dogs.

Step 1
Draw a rectangle for the body. Draw a triangle for the neck. The triangle should overlap the rectangle.

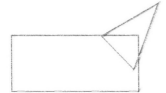

Step 2
Add a rectangle for the head. Draw a triangle for the eye and an arc for the nose.

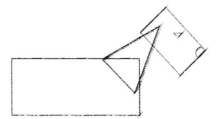

Step 3
Add four long rectangles for the legs.

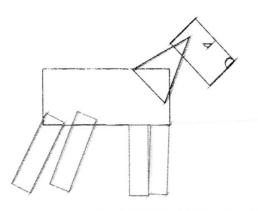

Step 4
Draw a crescent for the tail. Add two triangle ears.

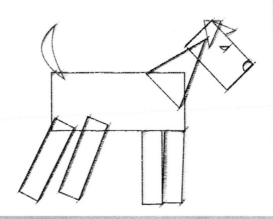

Step 5

Connect your shapes with a darker, sketchy line.

Step 6

Add short, sketchy lines for fur. Erase the lines you no longer need.

Step 7

Continue adding short lines to shade in the Airedale. Darken the eye and nose. Add a curved line over the eye. Smudge the lines with your finger.

American Shorthair Cat

The American shorthair is one of the most common cats in the world. It's easy to care for, friendly, and very healthy. Most American shorthairs are silver with black markings, but they can be many other colors.

Step 1

Draw an arc for the body and a circle for the head.

Step 2

Draw a circle for the muzzle. Add two triangles for the ears and a curved line for the tail.

Step 3

Draw two circles for the eyes and a triangle for the nose.

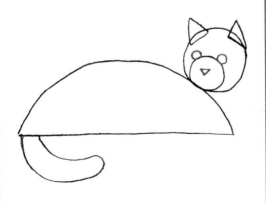

Step 4

Draw six ovals for the legs. Draw three ovals for the paws. The fourth leg and paw are hiding.

Step 5
Define the cat with a sketch line. Add two curved lines for the mouth.

Step 6
Erase the extra lines. Add details such as stripes, pupils, whiskers, and toes.

Step 7
Color your cat and add a background.

Burmese Cat

Some people say the Burmese looks like a "brick wrapped in silk" because of its sturdy body and soft fur. The Burmese is full of energy and often mischievous. It also loves being around people.

Step 1

Draw an oval for the body and a circle for the head.

Step 2

Draw circles for the eyes and muzzle. Add two triangles for the ears and one for the nose.

Step 3

Draw two ovals for the hind legs and two for the paws. Add a curved line for the tail.

Step 4

Draw two curved lines for the front legs and paws.

Step 5

Define the cat with a sketch line. Add two curved lines for the mouth and one for the chin.

Step 6

Erase the extra lines. Add details such as whiskers and toes.

Step 7

Color your cat and add a background.

Siberian Cat

The Siberian cat is energetic and full of surprises. Its glaring eyes and pointed ears make it seem dangerous. But it loves to play and can jump great distances.

Step 1

Draw a circle for the head and an oval for the body.

Step 2

Add two triangles for the ears. Draw an oval for the muzzle.

Step 3

Draw an oval for the eye. Add a triangle for the nose. Draw two curved lines for the neck.

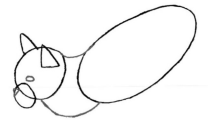

Step 4

Draw nine ovals for the legs and paws.

Step 5

Draw a curved line for the tail. Define the cat with a zigzag sketch line.

Step 6

Erase the extra lines. Add details such as a pupil, whiskers, toes, and fur.

Step 7

Color your cat and add a background.

Persian Cat

A fluffy white coat makes the Persian cat stand out from other cats. The Persian cat is sweet and gentle. Its short ears and big eyes make it look frightened, but as long as it feels comfortable and secure, it's happy.

Step 1

Draw a small circle inside a large circle for the body and the head.

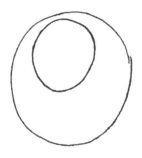

Step 2

Add two triangles for the ears. Draw two ovals for the eyes.

Step 3

Draw two ovals for the chest and one for the tail.

Step 4

Draw three rectangles for the legs and three for the paws. The fourth leg and paw are hiding.

Step 5

Define the cat with a zigzag sketch line. Add a triangle for the nose and two curved lines for the mouth.

Step 6

Erase the extra lines. Add details such as pupils and fur.

Step 7

Color your cat and add a background.

Angelfish

The black-striped angelfish is one of the most unique-looking aquarium fish. It seems to glide through the water without moving any fins, but its side fins push it along.

Step 1
Draw a trapezoid for the body. Add a small circle for the eye.

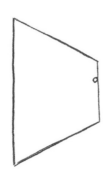

Step 2
Draw two arcs to complete the body.

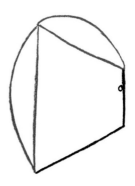

Step 3
Draw a rectangle and a trapezoid for the tail.

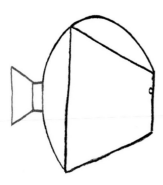

Step 4
Draw two ovals and two triangles for the fins. The top fin is a long, skinny triangle.

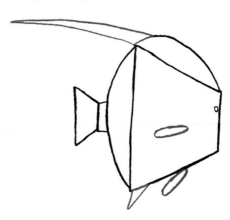

Step 5

Draw a curved line for the face. The angelfish has puckered lips. Define the fish with a sketch line.

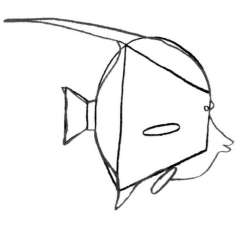

Step 6

Erase the extra lines. Add details such as curved lines for the stripes.

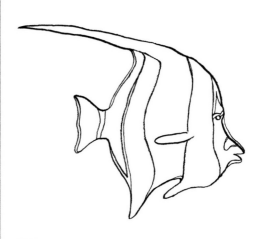

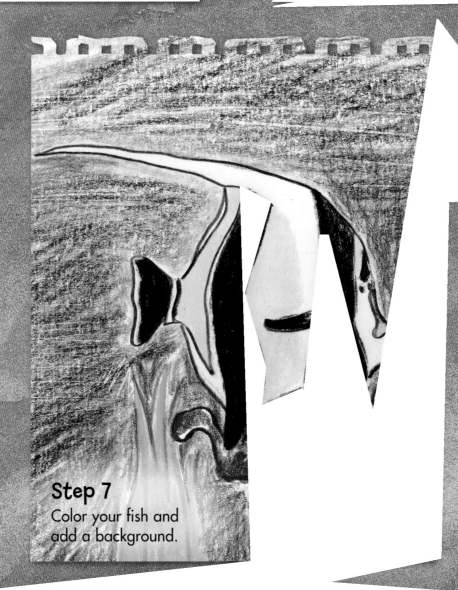

Step 7

Color your fish and add a background.

Blue Marlin

Blue on top and silver on the bottom, the blue marlin is a beautiful fish. It has long, pointed upper jaws that look like spears. It lives mostly in the Atlantic Ocean and can weigh up to 2,000 pounds (900 kilograms).

Step 1

Draw an oval for the body. Add two triangles for the upper and lower jaws.

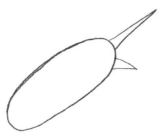

Step 2

Draw a small circle for the eye. Below the body draw a crescent for the tail.

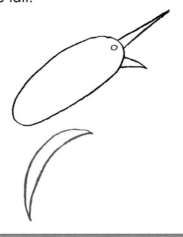

Step 3

Connect the body to the tail with two curved lines. Draw two curved lines for the fins.

Step 4

Draw two triangles for the bottom fins and a curved line for the large top fin.

Step 5
Finish the mouth with two zigzag lines. Define the fish with a sketch line.

Step 6
Erase the extra lines. Add details such as short lines on the top fin and a curved line along the marlin's side.

Step 7
Color your fish and add a background.

Bubble-Eye Goldfish

The bubble-eye goldfish makes a great pet because it's easy to care for. The bubble-eye is special because its eyes stick out from its head. They wobble around like big balloons as the goldfish swims.

Step 1

Draw an oval for the body. Draw two circles for the eyes. Add two dots for the pupils.

Step 2

Draw two large circles for the bubble eyes. The circles should overlap the fish.

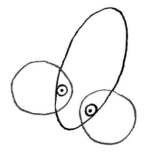

Step 3

Draw a curved line for the tail. Draw a diagonal line inside the tail.

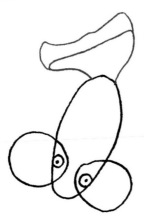

Step 4

Draw four ovals for the fins.

Step 5
Define the fish with a sketch line.

Step 6
Erase the extra lines. Connect the two bubble eyes with a curved line. Add details such as wavy lines for the scales.

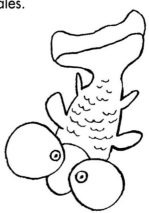

Step 7
Color your fish and add a background.

Largemouth Bass

The largemouth bass is a popular lake fish in the United States. It's usually green, with dark splotches that make a line down the side of its body. When it's hooked on a fishing line, it puts up a good fight.

Step 1

Draw an oval for the body. Add a small circle for the eye.

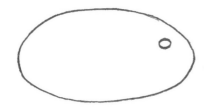

Step 2

Draw two circles and a triangle for the tail. Connect the body to the tail with two curved lines.

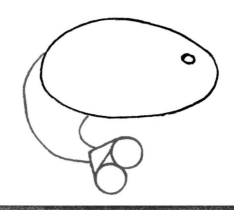

Step 3

Draw an arc and a triangle for the large mouth.

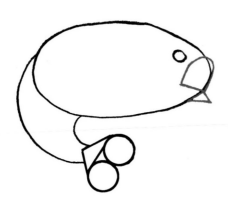

Step 4

Draw five curved lines for the fins. Add one tall arc for the side fin.

Step 5

Define the fish with a sketch line. The top fin has a curved sketch line. Add short lines to the top fin for the spines.

Step 6

Erase the extra lines. Add details such as curved lines for the gills.

Step 7

Color your fish and add a background.

Quarter Horse

Quarter horses have powerful muscles, small ears, and large eyes. Their backs are wide and sloping. Quarter horses are used for barrel racing, cargo carrying, and to tend and herd cattle. They come in 13 solid colors.

Step 1
Draw an oval for the head and a circle for the muzzle.

Step 2
Connect the head and the muzzle with two curved lines. Add two arcs for the eyes.

Step 3
Draw two long curving lines for the neck. Add a circle for the nostril and a diagonal line for the mouth.

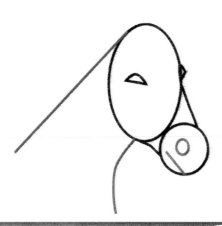

Step 4
Draw two triangles for ears. Add a circle and two curving lines along the face and below the ear for the bridle.

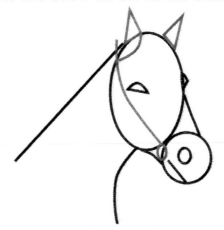

Step 5

Add short, wavy lines for the mane.
Add two curved lines and two
circles for the reins.

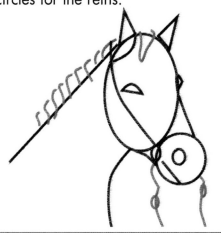

Step 6

Connect the shapes with a darker,
sketchy line. Draw a wavy heart for
the marking on the forehead. Begin
shading the horse.

Step 7

Shade in the horse using the side of your pencil.
Leave the heart marking white. Darken the eye,
nostril, and ears.

Clydesdale Horse

Clydesdales are very large horses with gentle personalities. They have well-defined markings on their faces. Clydesdales have four white socks, or bands, on their shins. They are usually brown, or brown with black manes and tails.

Step 1

Draw an oval for the body. Draw a big circle on each end of the oval.

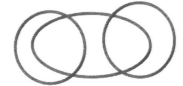

Step 2

Draw a circle for the head and a smaller circle for the muzzle. Connect the head and muzzle with two short lines. Draw two curving lines for the neck.

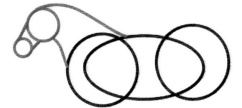

Step 3

Draw four ovals for the thighs. Add four circles for the knees.

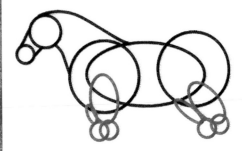

Step 4

Below the knees, add large trapezoids for the long hair on the horse's hooves. Add short lines for the mane.

Step 5

Draw two triangles for ears. Draw an arc for the eye and an oval for the nostril. Draw several ovals for the mane and a larger oval for the tail sprig decoration.

Step 6

Connect the shapes with a darker, sketchy line. Begin erasing the shapes inside. Add a diagonal line for the mouth. Draw a curved line for the marking on the horse's head.

Step 7

Shade in the horse using the side of your pencil. Add a short line inside the ovals for the mane decoration. Leave the hair on the hooves white.

Pinto Horse

Pintos were brought to North America by Spanish explorers. They have two color patterns: white with large, colored spots, or dark with white spots. *Pinto* means *painted* in Spanish.

Step 1

Draw a diagonal oval for the body. Add a circle at each end of the oval. Draw a circle for the head. Draw a small circle for the muzzle.

Step 2

Connect the muzzle, head, and body with three curving lines. Add an arc for the eye. Draw three ovals for the thighs. The fourth leg is hidden.

Step 3

Draw a circle for the nostril and a diagonal line for the mouth. Draw three rectangles, three circles, and three rectangles for the legs.

Step 4

Draw three circles at the bottoms of the rectangles. Draw three trapezoids for the hooves. Draw two triangles for ears.

Step 5

On the far side, draw a rectangle for the leg. Add a circle knee and a small rectangle for the shin. Add curved lines for the mane and tail.

Step 6

Connect the shapes with a darker, sketchy line. Begin erasing the shapes inside. Add curved lines for the pinto's spots. Shade in the mane and tail.

Step 7

Continue adding curved lines to the mane and tail. Shade in the pinto's spots. Leave some areas white. Shade in the nostril, eye, and hooves.

Thoroughbred Horse

Thoroughbreds have full chests and long, straight legs. They are very tall. Thoroughbreds are used for track racing, jumping, and pleasure riding. They eat corn, oats, bran, and carrots. Thoroughbreds come in solid colors, such as black and chestnut

Step 1

Draw a long oval for the body. Draw a circle at each end of the oval. Draw a circle for the head and a smaller circle for the muzzle.

Step 2

Connect the muzzle, head, and body with four curving lines. Draw an oval and a circle for the jockey. Add a circle for the horse's thigh.

Step 3

Draw three ovals for the jockey's arm and leg. Draw four rectangles for the horse's legs. Add four circles for the knees.

Step 4

Draw an arc for the jockey's hat. Draw four rectangles and four circles for the horse's legs. Add two triangles for ears. Draw an arc and an oval for the eye and the nostril.

Step 5

Draw four trapezoids for the hooves. Draw curved lines for the mane and the tail. Add a circle for the jockey's hand. Draw a rectangle and an oval for the boot.

Step 6

Connect the shapes with a darker, sketchy line. Begin erasing the shapes inside. Add a small circle and lines for the bridle and reins.

Step 7

Shade in the horse with the side of your pencil. Darken the mane, tail, eye, and nostril. Shade in the jockey's boot, shirt, and pants.

Jaguar

The jaguar is a large, powerful cat. It hunts in the darkness, sneaking up on its prey and then pouncing. It shows incredible balance as it bounces from rocks to branches in search of food or a place to sleep.

Step 1
Draw an oval and two circles for the body.

Step 2
Draw two circles for the head. Add two arcs for the ears.

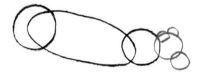

Step 3
Draw six ovals and four rectangles for the legs.

Step 4
Draw four circles for the paws. Add a wavy line for the tail.

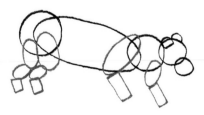

Step 5
Define the jaguar with a sketch line.

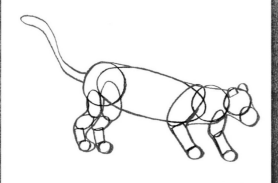

Step 6
Erase the extra lines. Add details such as whiskers, a nose, an eye, and wavy circles for the spots.

Step 7
Color your animal and add a background.

Spider Monkey

The spider monkey uses its long tail and strong hands to grab branches as it swings from tree to tree. It spends its whole life in the treetops, eating fruit, leaves, and seeds.

Step 1
Draw an oval for the body and a circle for the head. Add two circles for the shoulders.

Step 2
Draw three ovals for the legs. Draw four rectangles for the feet.

Step 3
Draw four rectangles and two circles for the arms. Draw two rectangles for the hands. Add a curved line for the tail.

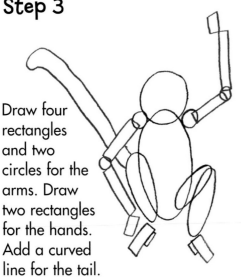

Step 4
Draw four ovals for the eyes. Draw two triangles for the ears and one for the nose. Add a circle for the mouth.

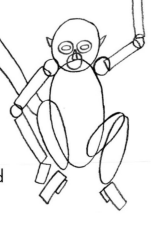

Step 5

Define the monkey with a zigzag sketch line. Add circles for the pupils. Draw short lines for the fingers and toes. Add a horizontal line for the mouth.

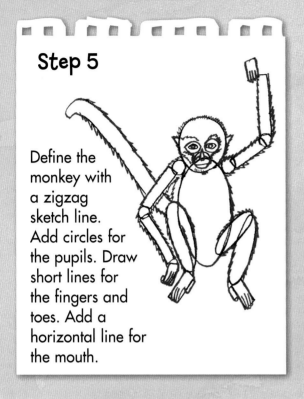

Step 6

Erase the extra lines. Add details such as fur and branches.

Step 7

Color your animal and add a background.

Scarlet Macaw

The scarlet macaw is one of the largest, most colorful parrots in the world. Bright red, yellow, and blue feathers cover its wings and long, slender tail. A curved bill helps the bird crack nuts and tear open fruit.

Step 1

Draw two ovals and a triangle for the wings. Draw an oval for the head.

Step 2

Connect the head to the wings with two curved lines. Add a skinny arc for the body.

Step 3

Draw a triangle and a curved line for the beak. Add a circle for the eye. Draw an oval around the eye.

Step 4

Draw long zigzag lines for the tail feathers. Add four diagonal lines for the tree branch.

Step 5

Define the parrot with a sketch line. Draw a diagonal line to separate the wings.

Step 6

Erase the extra lines. Add details such as zigzag lines for the feathers.

Step 7

Color your animal and add a background.

Sloth

The slow-moving sloth spends most of its life in the trees. It hangs upside down by its sharp, hook-like claws. Its fur often has bits of green in it because of the algae growing there. This coloring helps the sloth hide amongst the leaves.

Step 1
Draw an oval for the body. Add a circle for the head.

Step 2
Draw a smaller circle inside the head for the face. Add two circles for the shoulders.

Step 3
Draw four rectangles for the arms. Add two ovals and two rectangles for the legs.

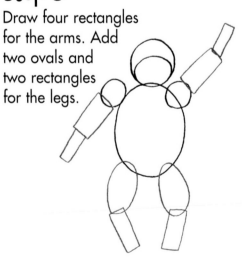

Step 4
Draw two ovals for the eyes. Draw a circle for the nose. Add three crescents and one triangle for the claws.

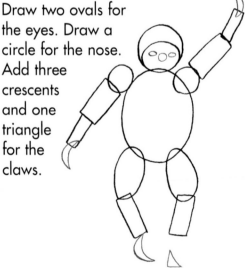

Step 5

Draw a curved line for the mouth. Define the sloth with a zigzag sketch line.

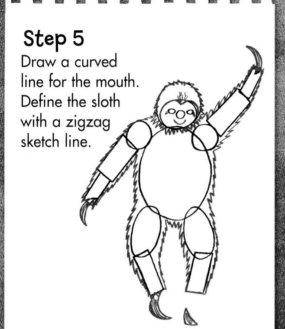

Step 6

Erase the extra lines. Add details such as pupils, nostrils, fur, and a tree branch.

Step 7

Turn your paper upside down. Color your animal and add a background.

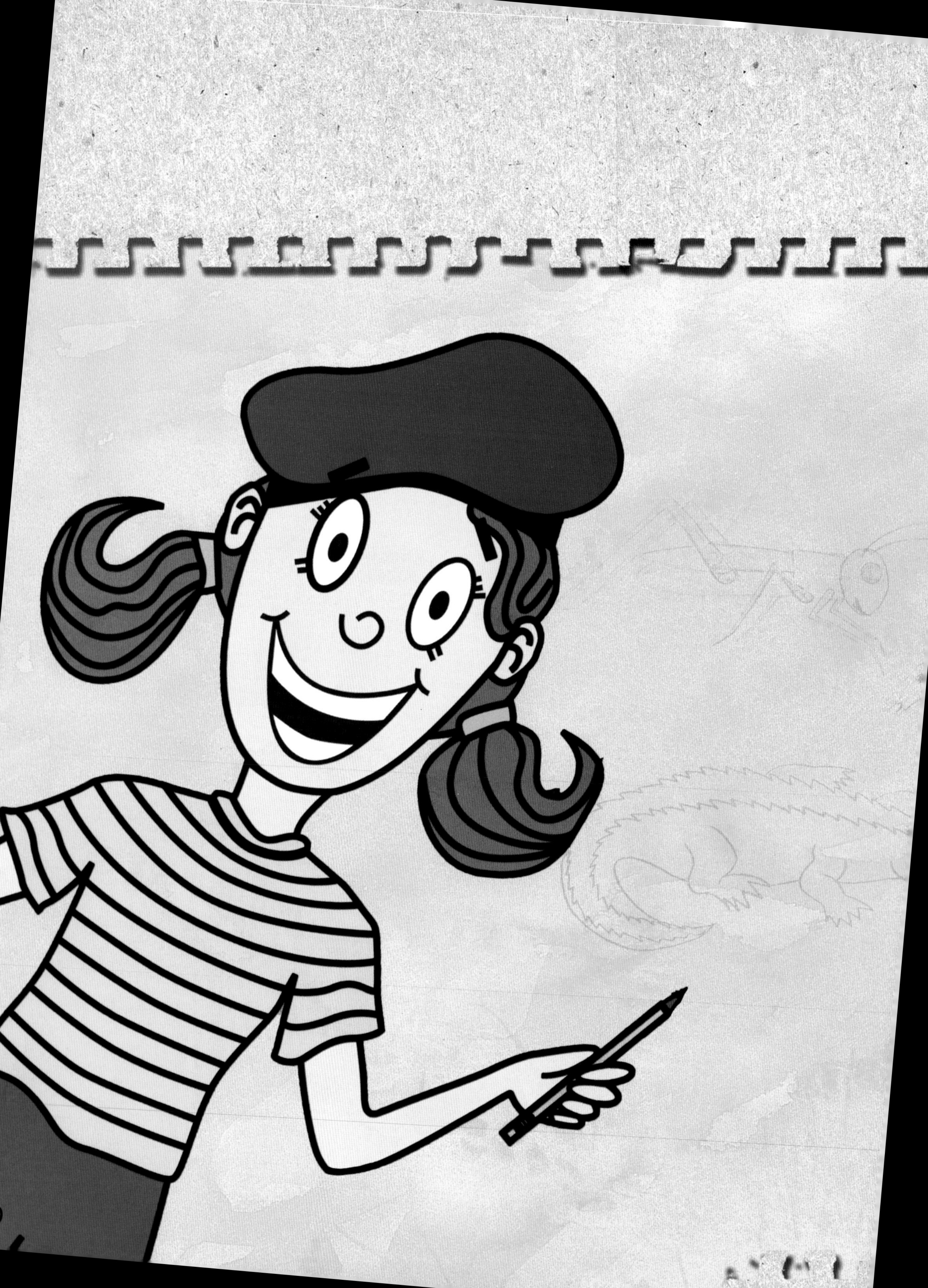

Chapter Two

BUGS

A

Ants are tiny workers with different jobs. Ants find food, dig tunnels, and even become soldiers. Ants work hard all through the summer. When winter comes, ants hide in warm spots deep in the earth. An ant has three sections: the head, the thorax, and the abdomen.

Step 1

Draw a circle for the head. Draw a circle for the eye. Add two curved lines for antennae.

Step 2

Draw an oval for the thorax.

Step 3

Draw a larger circle for the abdomen. Add a triangle for the end tip of the abdomen.

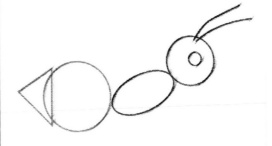

Step 4

Draw three zigzag lines for the legs on the near side. Draw all three legs in the middle section.

Step 5

Draw three zigzag lines for the legs on the far side. They should match the legs you've already drawn on the near side.

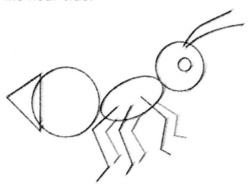

Step 6

Draw a curved line for the mouth. Trace over your lines and make them darker. Erase any lines you no longer need.

Step 7

Shade in the body with your pencil. Make the eye a darker shade than the rest of the ant.

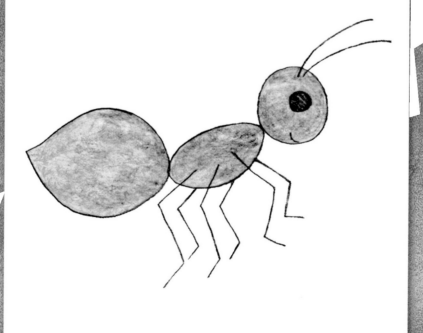

Dragonfly

Dragonflies live in warm climates. They are usually found near ponds and rivers. Dragonflies are very large. A full-grown dragonfly can be as large as an adult's hand!

Step 1
Draw a vertical guideline. This line will be erased. On the vertical guideline, draw an oval for the top part of the body.

Step 2
Draw an oval and a small circle for the head.

Step 3
Draw an oval for the bottom part of the body. Divide the oval on the top into two circles for the eyes. Add zigzag lines for the arms.

Step 4
Below the head, draw four ovals for the wings. Two ovals will be on each side of the body.

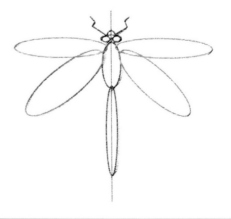

Step 5
Trace over the lines you want to keep.

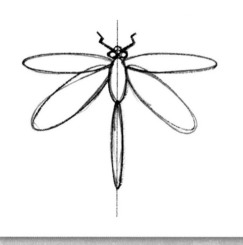

Step 6
Begin shading in the body. Leave some areas white for markings. Erase the lines you no longer need.

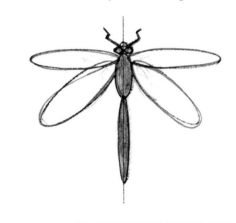

Step 7
Continue shading and add thin lines to the wings. Leave some areas white for markings.

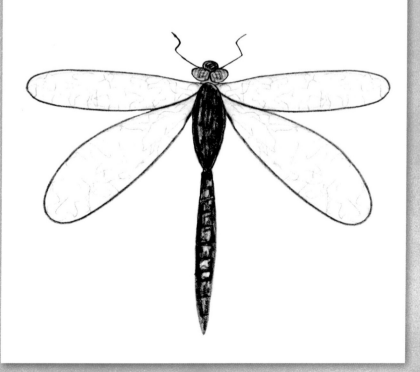

Grasshopper

The largest grasshopper can jump a distance of six feet (1.8 meters). Grasshoppers rub their long back legs together to make noise. These insects eat plants of all kinds.

Step 1

Draw an oval for the body. Overlap the oval with a square for the neck.

Step 2

Draw an oval for the head. Add a small circle for the eye. Draw two curved lines for the antennae.

Step 3

Draw two zigzag lines for the front legs. Draw two more zigzag lines for the middle legs.

Step 4

Draw two large zigzag lines for the back legs.

Step 5

Draw a horizontal line across the oval for the wings. Repeat the zigzag lines for the front, middle, and back legs, making the legs thick.

Step 6

Trace over the lines you want to keep. Add a curved line for the mouth. Erase the lines you no longer need.

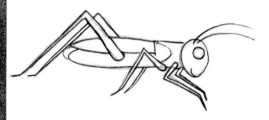

Step 7

Shade in the grasshopper using your pencil. Make the eye darker.

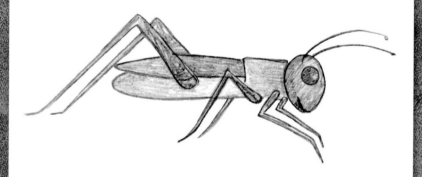

Ladybug

Ladybugs are a type of beetle. They are usually orange with black spots. Ladybugs keep plants healthy by getting rid of pests in the garden.

Step 1
Draw a circle for the body. Draw a vertical line down the center of the circle.

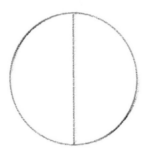

Step 2
Draw an oval for the head. Add two circles and a rectangle on the top of the head.

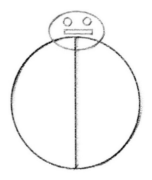

Step 3
Draw two curved lines for antennae.

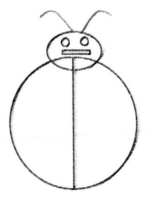

Step 4
Draw six short zigzag lines for legs. A ladybug has three legs on each side.

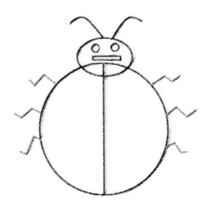

Step 5

Draw different-sized circles for spots on the body.

Step 6

Trace over the lines you want to keep. Erase the lines you no longer need. Begin shading with your pencil.

Step 7

Continue shading in the head, body, and spots. The spots on the ladybug's head should be lighter than the spots on its body. Darken the legs.

Monarch Butterfly

A monarch butterfly lays its eggs on the underside of milkweed plant leaves. Caterpillars hatch from the eggs and begin feeding on the plant. A caterpillar sheds its skin and creates a chrysalis. A monarch comes out of the chrysalis.

Step 1

Draw a small circle for the head. Draw two curved lines with rounded ends for antennae.

Step 2

Draw an oval for the top section of the body. Draw a longer oval for the bottom section of the body.

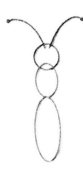

Step 3

Draw two long, curved lines for the wings. Start the lines between the circle and the oval.

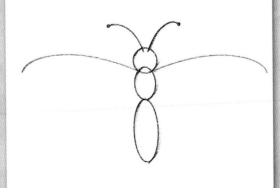

Step 4

Draw wavy lines down to the bottom of the long oval. The lines should curve like the top of a heart.

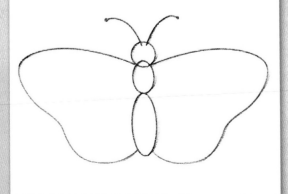

Step 5

Repeat the curved and wavy lines on the inside of the wing. Add a curved line like a rainbow across the wings.

Step 6

Add curved lines inside the wings for designs. Draw small circles and ovals on the wings, body, and head. Erase the lines you no longer need.

Step 7

Continue shading the butterfly. Make the outside edge of the wings darker. Leave the spots white.

Wasp

Wasps sting and kill insect pests. Wasps love
to visit picnics and eat trash, such as rotten fruit.
Wasps are black and yellow.

Step 1

Draw a circle for the smaller part
of the body.

Step 2

Draw an oval for the head.
Draw a large circle for the eye.
Add two curved lines for antennae.

Step 3

Draw a larger oval for the larger
part of the body.

Step 4

Draw two large ovals for the wings.

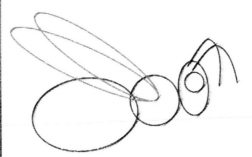

Step 5

Draw three zigzag lines for the legs. Start drawing the zigzag lines at the middle circle.

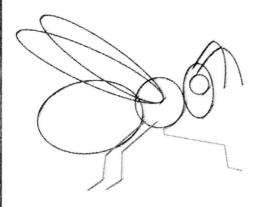

Step 6

Trace over the lines. Erase half of the wing on the far side. Erase the lines you no longer need.

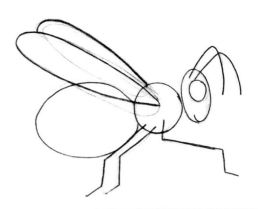

Step 7

Add curved lines for stripes on the end section of the body. Make a pattern by shading in the stripes. Continue shading. Add thin wing lines.

Bedbug

Bedbugs have flat bodies and are reddish-brown. They can live for months without food. Bedbugs live in warm, dry places. They bite birds, bats, dogs, and even people!

Step 1
Draw a medium-sized circle for the middle section of the bedbug.

Step 2
Draw a small circle for the head.

Step 3
Draw a larger oval for the back section of the body. The oval and the middle circle should overlap.

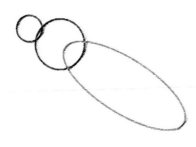

Step 4
Draw two diagonal lines for the legs on each side of the oval. Add short lines for the feet.

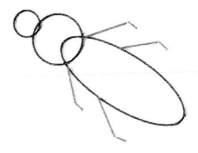

Step 5

Add two diagonal lines for the front legs. Add short lines for the back legs. Draw two curved lines for the antennae.

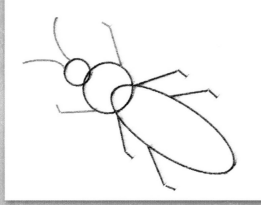

Step 6

Trace over the lines. When tracing, curve the middle circle like the letter C. Sketch a pointed tip at the end of the oval for the body. Erase the lines you no longer need.

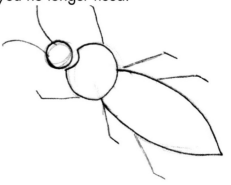

Step 7

Continue to darken the lines. Shade in the bedbug with your pencil. Shade the head darker than the rest of the body.

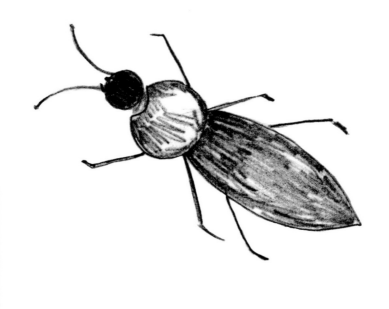

Pond Skater

Pond skaters walk on the surface of the water. They are very light. A pond skater's body has a protective coat of fur on it to keep the water away. The fur is so thin you can't see it.

Step 1

Draw a long, skinny oval for the body. Draw a small rectangle for the head.

Step 2

At the bottom of the rectangle, add two circles for the eyes. Draw two curved lines for antennae.

Step 3

Draw six zigzag lines for the legs. Four of the legs begin at the oval. Two of the legs begin at the rectangle head.

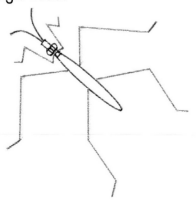

Step 4

Draw short lines across the end of the long oval.

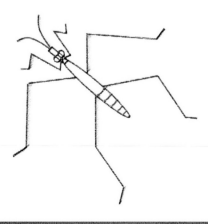

Step 5
Draw thin circles around each foot to show the water.

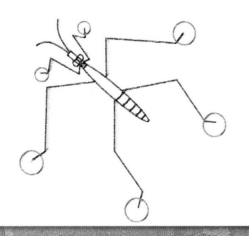

Step 6
Trace over the lines you want to keep. Erase the lines you no longer need.

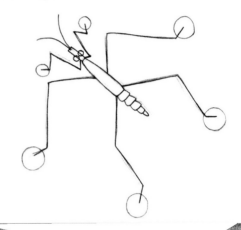

Step 7
Shade in the pond skater using the side of your pencil.

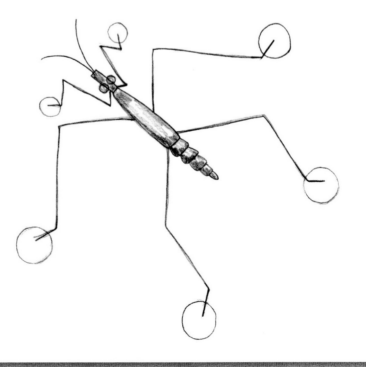

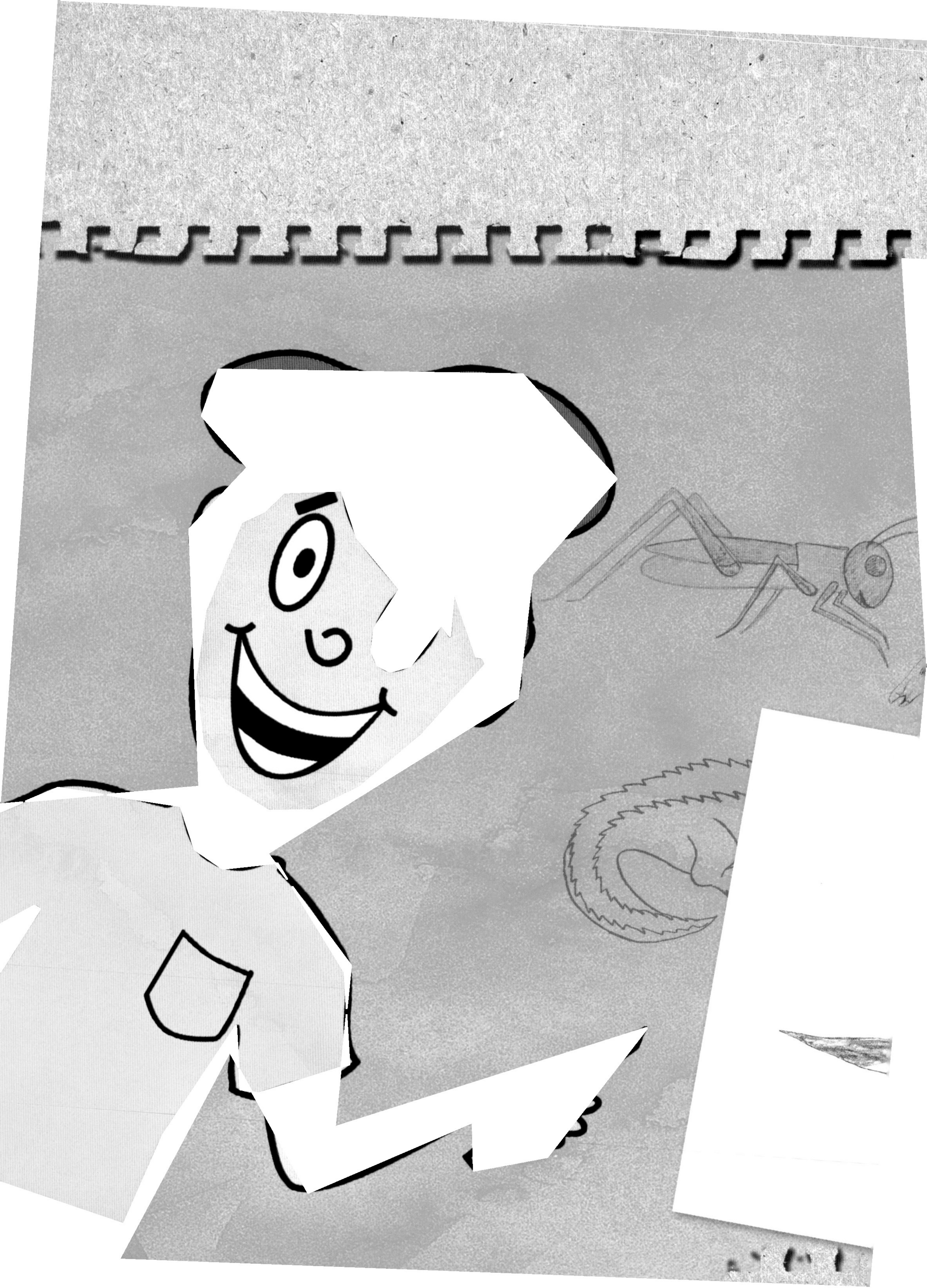

Chapter Three

DINOSAURS

Compsognathus (KOMP-sog-NAY-thus)

Compsognathus was one of the smallest dinosaurs. It looked a little like a bird, but it had a lizard-like tail. Compsognathus had three-toed feet. It ate insects and

Step 1
Draw an oval for the body. Draw a circle for the head.

Step 2
Connect the circle and the oval with two curved lines for the neck.

Step 3
Draw a circle for an eye. Add two triangles for the beak. Draw a zigzag line for sharp teeth. Add a long crescent for the tail.

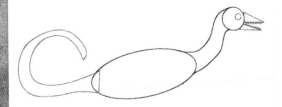

Step 4
Draw a large oval for the back thigh. Add an oval and two rectangles for the shin and foot. Draw one triangle claw. Draw a square and a rectangle for the other shin and foot. Draw three triangles for claws.

Step 5

Draw two smaller ovals for the front upper arms. Add two squares and two rectangles for forearms. Add four triangles for the claws.

Step 6

Draw a darker, sketchy line around the shapes. Erase the lines you no longer want. Begin adding oval spots on the back.

Step 7

Compsognathus was darker on its back than on its tummy. Shade in the oval spots with your pencil. Shade around the eye. It will look as if Compsognathus is wearing a mask.

Diplodocus (die-PLOH-dah-kus)

Diplodocus was a giant dinosaur. It was as long as two school buses put together! Diplodocus had nostrils on top of its head and had very weak teeth. It was a plant-eater.

Step 1
Draw an oval for the body and an oval for the head.

Step 2
Connect the ovals with two curved lines for the neck.

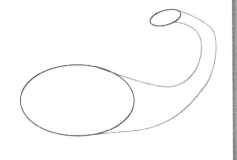

Step 3
Draw a circle for the eye. Draw a horizontal line for the mouth. Draw two curving lines for the tail.

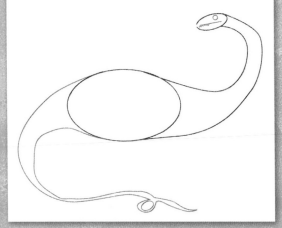

Step 4
Draw an oval for the back thigh. Add two rectangles for shins. Draw two rectangles for feet.

Step 5

Draw an oval for the front thigh. Add two rectangles for shins. Draw two rectangles for feet. Add two triangles for claws.

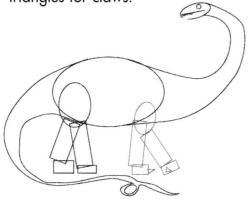

Step 6

Draw a darker, sketchy line around the shapes. Erase the lines you no longer want. Begin adding wavy lines for the tough skin.

Step 7

Shade in with the side of your pencil. Diplodocus had thick, tough skin, so use a lot of wavy lines.

Pachycephalosaurus (PACK-ee-cef-AH-loh-SORE-us)

Pachycephalosaurus had a huge, dome-shaped head. Its head was covered with spikes. It had two powerful back legs used for running and walking. Pachycephalosaurus had short arms. It was a plant-eater.

Step 1
Draw an oval for the body. Draw an oval for the head. Draw a circle for the eye. Add two arcs for the beak. The top arc is larger than the bottom arc.

Step 2
Connect the ovals with two curved lines for the neck. Pachycephalosaurus had bumps all over its head. Draw circles and ovals for the bumps.

Step 3
Draw a large oval for the thigh and an oval for the shin. Draw an oval for the other thigh.

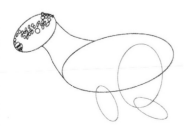

Step 4
Draw two rectangles for shins. On the near side, draw another rectangle. Draw two triangles on each side to make feet.

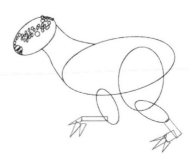

Step 5

Draw an oval for the upper arm. Draw two rectangles for the forearms. Add zigzag lines for claws. Draw a triangle tail.

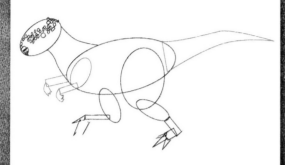

Step 6

Draw a darker, sketchy line around the shapes. Erase the lines you no longer want. Begin shading darker spots on the back.

Step 7

Continue shading the spots. Shade in the eye and the bumps on the head.

Spinosaurus (SPIE-noh-SORE-us)

Spinosaurus is called *spiny lizard* because it had large spines on its back. The spines could reach up to 6 feet (1.8 meters) tall. Spinosaurus was a meat-eater. It had a powerful jaw with sharp teeth like a crocodile's.

Step 1
Draw two circles side by side for the body. One circle should be larger than the other. Add a circle for the head.

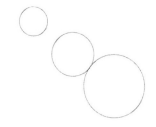

Step 2
Connect the three circles with curving lines for the neck and body. Draw two rectangles for the snout. Draw a small circle for the eye.

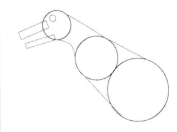

Step 3
Draw two ovals for the upper arms. Draw two rectangles for the forearms. Add zigzag lines for the claws.

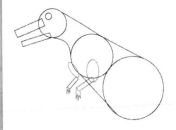

Step 4
Draw a large oval for the thigh. Draw an oval for the knee. Add two rectangles for the shin and foot. Draw a zigzag line for the claws. Add a triangle tail.

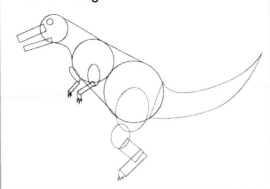

Step 5

Draw an oval for the other thigh. Add an oval for the knee and two rectangles for the shin and foot. Add a zigzag line for claws. Draw an arc for the spine.

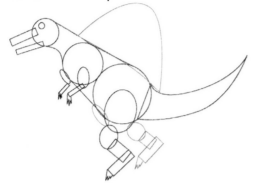

Step 6

Add a zigzag line for sharp teeth. Draw a darker, sketchy line around the shapes. Erase the lines you no longer want.

Step 7

Add long triangles inside the spine. Shade them in with your pencil. Add small circles for scales.

Stegosaurus (STEG-oh-SORE-us)

Stegosaurus' back legs were longer than its front legs. It had diamond-shaped plates on its back and spikes on its tail. Stegosaurus was a plant-eater.

Step 1
Draw an oval for the body. The oval should be tilted higher in the back. Draw an oval for the head.

Step 2
Connect the head and the body with two curving lines for the neck. Draw a circle for the eye. Add two small triangles for the beak.

Step 3
Draw two ovals for the arms. Add two rectangles for the shins.

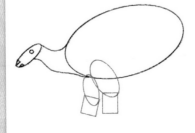

Step 4
Draw two ovals for the thighs. Draw two rectangles for the shins. Add a triangle tail.

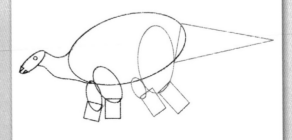

Step 5

Draw small diamonds on top of the neck. Draw larger diamonds on the back. The diamonds should get smaller again as you draw farther down the tail. Add three triangles on the tail.

Step 6

Draw a darker, sketchy line around the shapes. Erase the lines you no longer want. When tracing, begin rounding the points of the diamonds. Add small arcs on the feet for claws.

Step 7

Shade in the Stegosaurus with the side of your pencil. Darken the eye. Add dark and light shadows on the spikes.

Triceratops (trie-SAIR-ah-TOPS)

Triceratops looked a little like a rhinoceros. It had three horns and a beak. Triceratops looked fierce—but it ate plants instead of other animals.

Step 1
Draw an oval for the body. Draw an oval for the head.

Step 2
Draw an arc for the eye. Add two triangles for the beak. Connect the beak to the head with two short lines. Connect the head and the body with two curving lines for the neck.

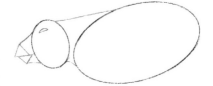

Step 3
Add a triangle between the head and the body. The triangle is the crest. Draw two ovals for the thigh and the arm.

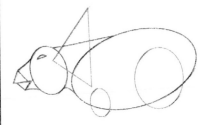

Step 4
Add four rectangles for the shins. Draw four circles for the feet.

Step 5

Draw three triangles for horns on Triceratops' head. Two horns are long and slender triangles. The third horn is a smaller triangle. Draw a triangle for the tail. Add a curved line for the mouth.

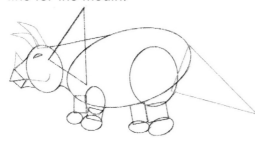

Step 6

Draw a darker, sketchy line around the shapes. Draw a wavy line along the back of the crest. Erase the lines you no longer want. Begin shading the crest with diagonal lines.

Step 7

Continue shading. The crest has darker shadows because it is bumpy. Add wavy lines around the mouth. Add lines around the eye and shade it darker.

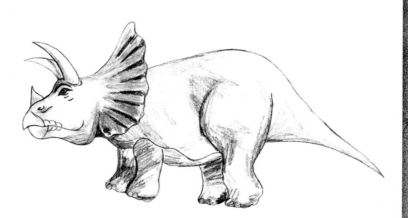

Tyrannosaurus rex (tie-RAN-oh-SORE-us REX)

Tyrannosaurus rex was one of the largest two-legged dinosaurs. It had a massive, powerful jaw with very large teeth. It had two strong back legs and two small arms. T. rex was so heavy, it could run only for a short distance.

Step 1
Draw an oval for the body. Draw a circle for the head.

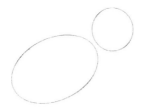

Step 2
Connect the head and the body with two curved lines for the neck. Add a circle for the eye. Draw two rectangles and one triangle for the powerful jaws. Add a zigzag line for large, sharp teeth.

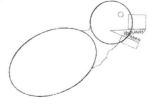

Step 3
Draw an oval for the arm. Add two rectangles to the oval. Draw zigzag lines for claws.

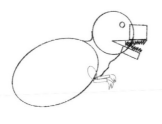

Step 4
Draw an oval for the thigh. Add a smaller oval for the shin. Draw a rectangle for the foot.

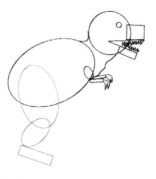

Step 5

Draw an oval for the other thigh. Add an oval for the shin. Draw a rectangle for the foot. Add a triangle tail.

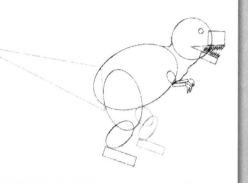

Step 6

Draw a darker, sketchy line around the shapes. Erase the lines you no longer want. Begin adding curved lines for T. rex's rough skin.

Step 7

Shade in with the side of your pencil. Darken the eye and add curved lines around the eye.

Velociraptor (vel-LOS-ih-RAP-tore)

This fast-running dinosaur was a meat-eater. It was only six feet (two meters) long. Velociraptor had a long snout and very sharp teeth. Some people believe this dinosaur was very intelligent.

Step 1
Draw a circle for the body. Draw an oval for the head. Draw two triangles for the jaws.

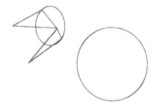

Step 2
Connect the circle and the oval with two curved lines for the neck. Draw an arc for the eye. Add a diagonal line for the jaw.

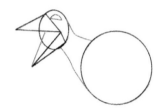

Step 3
Draw two ovals for the arms. Add two rectangles for the forearms. Draw two circles for the hands. Add zigzag lines for the claws.

Step 4
Draw two ovals for thighs. Draw two rectangles for shins. Draw two rectangles for feet. On the near side, draw a small square for the toe. Draw three triangles for claws on each foot.

Step 5

Draw three zigzag lines for teeth. Add a triangle tail.

Step 6

Draw a darker, sketchy line around the shapes. Erase the lines you no longer want. Begin shading a zigzag pattern on the back.

Step 7

Continue shading in the zigzag pattern. Shade in the mouth, eye, and claws. On the far side, add a triangle for another claw on the foot.

Chapter Four

Cool Stuff

Embarrassed Face

When you are embarrassed, your cheeks turn red. Your eyes grow large and round. When you walk into the wrong classroom by mistake or get called on by the teacher and forget the answer, you probably have an embarrassed face.

Step 1
Draw an oval for the head. Draw two guidelines. One of your guidelines should be horizontal, and the other should be vertical.

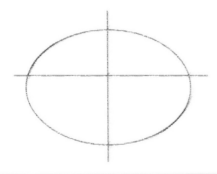

Step 2
On the horizontal guideline, draw two large ovals for eyes. Add two smaller ovals for the pupils.

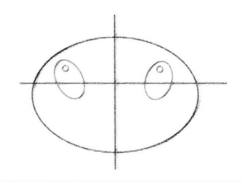

Step 3
Draw two wavy lines for eyebrows. On the vertical guideline, draw a curved line for the nose.

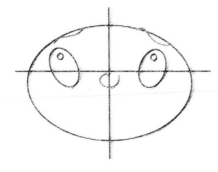

Step 4
Draw an oval for the mouth. Inside the oval, draw two curved lines for the top and bottom lip. Draw a horizontal line and short vertical lines for the teeth.

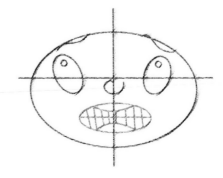

Step 5

Draw two arcs for the ears. Add squiggly lines inside of the ears. Draw wavy lines for curly hair.

Step 6

Continue adding wavy lines for hair. Trace over the lines you want to keep. Erase the guidelines and other lines you don't need.

Step 7

Add two vertical lines for the neck. Add curved lines below the eyes for cheeks. Shade in the cheeks with your pencil. Shade in the hair, eyes, and eyebrows.

Angry Face

When you are angry, your eyes narrow sharply. Your face looks pinched. If the neighbor kid breaks your favorite toy or your sister won't get out of your room, you probably have an angry face.

Step 1
Draw an oval for the head. Draw two guidelines. One of your guidelines should be horizontal, and the other should be vertical.

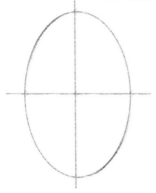

Step 2
On the horizontal guideline, draw two ovals for eyes. Add two small circles for the pupils.

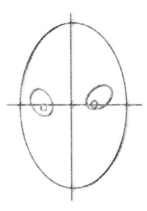

Step 3
Draw a diagonal line on top of both ovals. Draw two wavy lines for eyebrows. The eyebrows should be tilted downward.

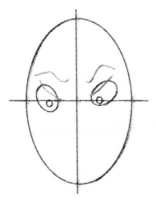

Step 4
On the vertical guideline, draw a curved line for the nose. Draw a wavy line for the frown. Draw two arcs for the ears. Add squiggly lines inside the ears.

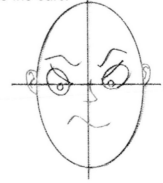

Step 5
Draw a lot of wavy lines for the hair.

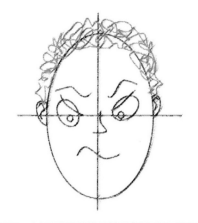

Step 6
Continue adding wavy lines for hair.
Trace over the lines you want to keep.
Erase the guidelines and other lines
you don't need.

Step 7
Erase the tops of the oval eyes. Add two vertical
lines for the neck. Continue shading in the hair,
eyes, and eyebrows.

Excited Face

When you are excited, your eyes might grow wide. A big smile might appear on your face. If you're going on a fun trip or to a friend's birthday party, you probably have an excited face.

Step 1

Draw an oval for the head. Draw two guidelines. One of your guidelines should be horizontal, and the other should be vertical.

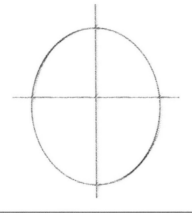

Step 2

Draw two large, oval eyes on the horizontal guideline. Draw two small ovals inside the eyes for pupils. Add two short, curved lines for eyebrows.

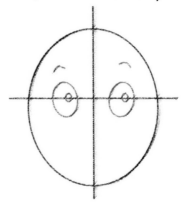

Step 3

On the vertical guideline, draw the letter c for the nose. Draw two curved lines for the smile. The smile should look like an arc.

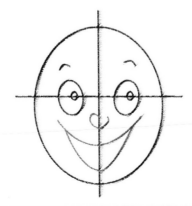

Step 4

Draw two curved lines for the top and bottom teeth. Add small curved lines for the corners of the mouth.

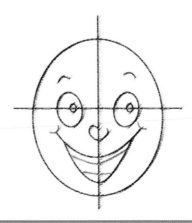

Step 5

On the horizontal guideline, draw two arcs for ears. Add squiggly lines inside the ears. Draw zigzag lines for hair.

Step 6

Trace over the lines you want to keep. Erase the guidelines and other lines you don't need.

Step 7

Draw two vertical lines for the neck. Use your pencil to shade in the mouth, hair, and eyes.

Scared Face

When you are scared, your mouth turns downward. Your eyebrows are raised with fear. When you listen to a ghost story or hear a bump in the night, you probably have a scared face.

Step 1
Draw an oval for the head. Draw two guidelines. One of your guidelines should be horizontal, and the other should be vertical.

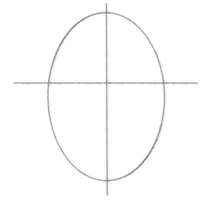

Step 2
On the horizontal guideline, draw two large ovals for eyes. Add two small ovals in the eyes for pupils.

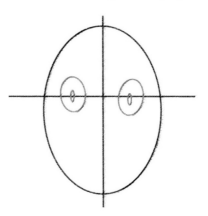

Step 3
Draw two diagonal lines for eyebrows. The eyebrows should tilt upward. On the vertical guideline, draw a curved line for the nose.

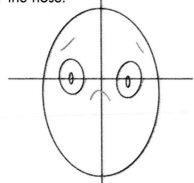

Step 4
Draw a rectangle for the mouth. Draw two arcs for ears. Add squiggly lines inside the ears.

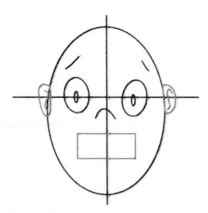

Step 5

Draw dizzy lines for hair. Add wavy lines for the mouth and top row of teeth. Draw the top of a heart for the tongue.

Step 6

Continue adding dizzy lines for hair. Trace over the lines you want to keep. Erase the guidelines and other lines you don't need.

Step 7

Draw two vertical lines for the neck. Continue shading in the hair with dizzy lines. Shade in the mouth, eyes, and eyebrows. Add short, curved lines for eyelashes.

The Flapper Dress

Flappers were fashionable, free-spirited women who danced the night away at jazz clubs in the late 1920s. They wore short dresses without much shape and no sleeves. Flapper dresses often had beads, sequins, or feathers.

Step 1

Draw an oval for the head and a rectangle for the dress.

Step 2

Draw two vertical lines for the neck. Add an arc for the hat. Draw two diagonal lines for the neckline of the dress.

Step 3

Draw a horizontal line for the slip beneath the dress. Add two curved lines for the sash. Draw diagonal lines for the fringes.

Step 4

Draw two diagonal lines for the hat ribbon. Add wavy lines for the hair.

Step 5

Define the hat and dress with a sketch line. Draw three rectangles for the arms. Draw two rectangles for the legs. Add two arcs for the hands.

Step 6

Erase the extra lines. Add details such as a face, a necklace, a feather boa, and shoes.

Step 7

Color your person and add a background.

Black Leather Jacket

In the 1950s, many young men followed the look of such stars as James Dean and Elvis Presley. The "rebel" look included blue jeans, a tight white t-shirt, and a black leather jacket. Some men also wore penny loafers and slicked back their hair.

Step 1

Draw a rectangle for the body. Add an oval for the head.

Step 2

Draw two vertical lines for the neck. Draw four ovals for the arms.

Step 3

Draw five rectangles for the jeans. Draw two ovals for the shoes.

Step 4

Draw two triangles for the collar. Add a curved line for the jacket zipper. Draw an oval for the hair.

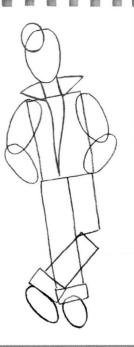

Step 5

Define the outfit with a sketch line. Draw two trapezoids for the hands. Add a curved line for the ear and the rest of the hair.

Step 6

Erase the extra lines. Add details such as a face, pockets, and a zipper on the jeans.

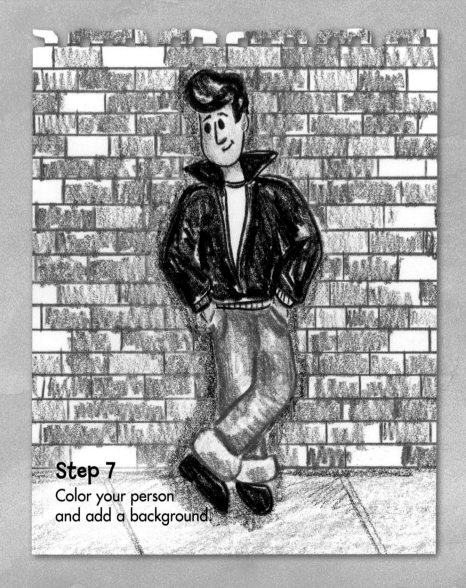

Step 7

Color your person and add a background.

Bell-Bottoms

In the late 1960s and early '70s, a lot of young men and women wore bell-bottom jeans. These jeans flared wide at the ankle to create a unique look.

Step 1

Draw a rectangle for the body. Add an oval for the head.

Step 2

Draw two vertical lines for the neck. Draw two rectangles for the legs. Add a crescent for the hair.

Step 3

Draw four rectangles for the arms. Draw two rectangles for the hands. Add two trapezoids for the bell-bottoms.

Step 4

Draw three triangles for the collar. Add two arcs and two rectangles for the shoes.

Step 5

Define the outfit with a sketch line. Define the hair with a wavy sketch line for the curly perm. Add two diagonal lines for the hands.

Step 6

Erase the extra lines. Add details such as a face, glasses, a mustache, and an oval for the belt buckle.

Step 7

Color your person and add a background.

The "Bar" Suit

In 1947, designer Christian Dior introduced a new look for women called the "Bar" suit. It included a full skirt and a fitted jacket with a tight waist. With World War II finally over, people celebrated life again by wearing fancy styles.

Step 1
Draw an arc for the shoulders and an oval for the head.

Step 2
Draw a triangle and a trapezoid for the body.

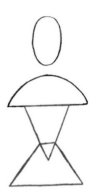

Step 3
Draw two vertical lines for the neck. Add a trapezoid for the skirt.

Step 4
Draw two triangles for the collar. Draw four ovals for the arms.

Step 5

Define the outfit with a sketch line. Draw two trapezoids for the hands. Add a vertical line down the middle of the jacket.

Step 6

Erase the extra lines. Add details such as a hat, a face, and boots. Draw diagonal and vertical lines for the pleats in the skirt.

Step 7

Color your person and add a background.

Sea Serpent

The sea serpent lives within the depths of large lakes and oceans. With its scaly skin, wing-like flippers, and snake-like tail, the sea serpent looks like a huge underwater dragon.

Step 1

Draw two triangles for the snout. Add two wavy lines for the body.

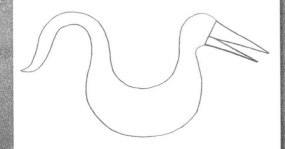

Step 2

Draw two arcs for the eyes and two arcs for the flippers.

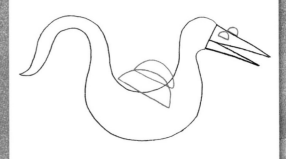

Step 3

Draw one zigzag line for the teeth. Add another zigzag line on the head and neck for the spikes.

Step 4

Draw wavy lines for the scales. Add small circles for the pupils.

Step 5

Define the monster with a sketch line. Define the flipper with a zigzag line.

Step 6

Erase the extra lines. Add details such as scales on the flippers.

Step 7

Color your monster and add a background.

Cyclops

A cyclops is easy to spot. A cyclops is a giant with just one eye—right in the middle of his forehead. He usually lives in caves and feeds on animals and people.

Step 1

Draw an arc for the head. Draw a rectangle for the body.

Step 2

Draw a rectangle for the legs. Add two ovals for the feet. Draw three circles for the eye.

Step 3

Draw two vertical lines for the arms and one for the legs. Add 10 ovals for the fingers and 10 for the toes.

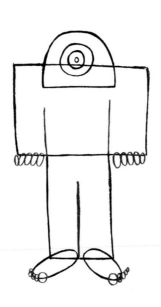

Step 4

Draw two crescents for the ears and one for the mouth.

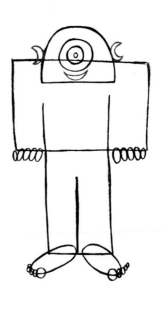

Step 5

Define the monster with a sketch line. Define the pants with two zigzag lines.

Step 6

Erase the extra lines. Add details such as hair, eyelashes, and teeth.

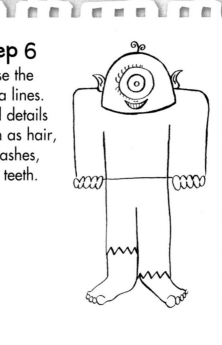

Step 7

Color your monster and add a background.

Bogeyman

The bogeyman sometimes hides in the bedrooms of naughty kids. He is always changing shape. Sometimes he has horns, fangs, or a long, spiky tail.

Step 1

Draw a trapezoid for the body and a triangle for the head. Add two circles for the eyes.

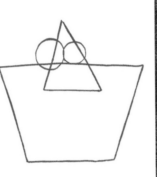

Step 2

Draw a rectangle for the legs and a circle for the stomach. Define the legs with a vertical line. Add two small circles for the pupils.

Step 3

Draw two ovals for the feet. Add eight ovals for the fingers. Add eight ovals for the toes.

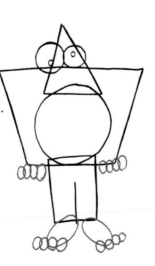

Step 4

Draw two crescents for the horns. Draw a triangle for the mouth. Add an oval for the nose.

Step 5
Define the monster with a zigzag sketch line.

Step 6
Erase the extra lines. Add details such as body hair and fangs.

Step 7
Color your monster and add a background.

Werewolf

The werewolf seems like a normal person by day. But when a full moon rises, fur starts growing all over his face and body. Sharp fangs jut out from behind his lips, and his howl fills the night air.

Step 1
Draw an oval for the head. Draw an arc for the shoulders. Add a square for the body.

Step 2
Draw four rectangles for the legs. Add two ovals for the feet. Draw two arcs for the hands.

Step 3
Draw eight triangles for the claws. Draw two circles and a triangle for the snout. Add two ovals for the eyes. Draw a square for the mouth.

Step 4
Draw two crescents for the ears. Draw a triangle for the nose. Add two arcs for the eyebrows.

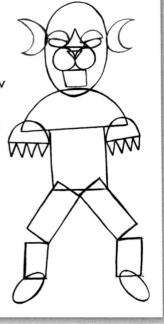

Step 5

Define the monster with a sketch line. Draw zigzag lines for the hair and the ripped pants.

Step 6

Erase the extra lines. Add details such as whiskers and the insides of the ears.

Step 7

Color your monster and add a background.

Vampire

The sun sets, and the vampire rises from his coffin. Vampires have long fangs and wear black capes. They lurk in the shadows, looking for a neck to bite. Some vampires can turn themselves into bats or wolves.

Step 1

Draw one oval for the head and one for the body. Add six rectangles for the arms and legs. Add two ovals for the eyes.

Step 2

Draw two arcs for the hands. Draw two ovals for the feet. Draw two vertical lines for the neck. Add a horizontal line for the mouth.

Step 3

Draw two triangles and a circle for the bow tie. Add two zigzag lines for the claws. Add two crescents for the ears.

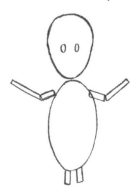

Step 4

Draw curved lines for the nose and the hair. Add two arcs for the eyebrows. Draw two triangles for the fangs.

Step 5

Draw a wavy line for the wings. Add a trapezoid for the cape. Add a zigzag line for the body hair. Define the monster with a sketch line.

Step 6

Erase the extra lines. Add details such as hair and wing folds.

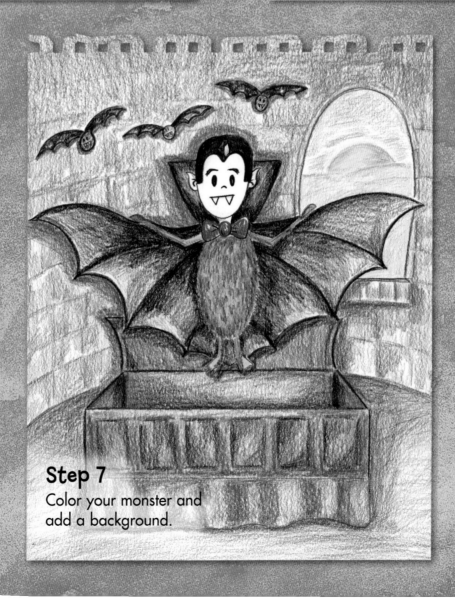

Step 7

Color your monster and add a background.

Alien

People come in all shapes, sizes, and colors— so do aliens! Aliens are beings from places beyond our planet. This alien has a thin body with a human shape, but its large eyes and huge, egg-shaped head make it stand out.

Step 1

Draw an oval for the head. Draw one rectangle for the neck and one for the body.

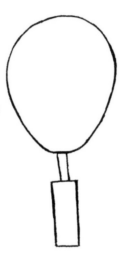

Step 2

Draw four rectangles for the arms. Add two ovals and a triangle for each hand. Draw two ovals for the eyes.

Step 3

Draw two arcs for the legs. Draw two ovals for the feet. Add a horizontal line for the mouth.

Step 4

Draw two trapezoids for the mouth. Add four triangles for the claws. Draw a triangle for the shirt neckline.

Step 5
Define the monster with a sketch line.

Step 6
Erase the extra lines. Add details such as teeth. Draw curved lines to define the eyes.

Step 7
Color your monster and add a background.

Pink Cadillac

The pink Cadillac was designed to be eye-catching. The Cadillac looked like a pink jet plane cruising down the road. It was more expensive than a family car because of its convertible top. It was created to be a luxury car.

Step 1

Draw a thin rectangle. Draw a horizontal line across the rectangle. Draw a vertical line down the center of the rectangle.

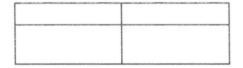

Step 2

Draw a vertical line near the front of the car. Label the sections with the numbers one, two, and three. In sections one and three, draw circles for the back and front wheels.

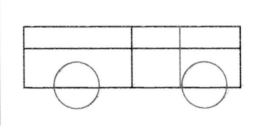

Step 3

In section two, draw a short vertical line down the center. The line should stop at the horizontal line. In section one, draw two horizontal lines. The top horizonal line should be slightly outside of the rectangle. Draw two circles inside the wheels.

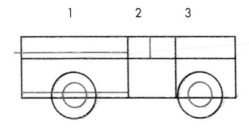

Step 4

In section two, draw a diagonal line for the front window. In section one, draw a curved line for the back of the car. In section three, add a small curved line for the hood. Add two small circles inside the wheels.

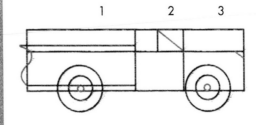

Step 5

In section one, draw a long, slender diamond for the rear car light. In section two, draw a vertical rectangle for the mirror. In section three, draw a rectangle for the bumper.

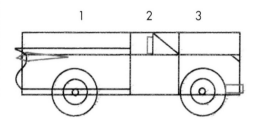

Step 6

Trace over the shapes with a darker, sketchy line. When tracing, watch how the lines overlap the wheels. Draw a diagonal line above the front wheel. Erase the top half of both wheels. Begin shading in the tires. Erase the lines you no longer need.

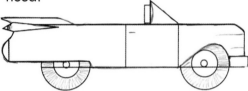

Step 7

Add details. Draw a small rectangle for a door handle. Continue shading in the tires. Shade in the front and back bumper, rear light, and front window.

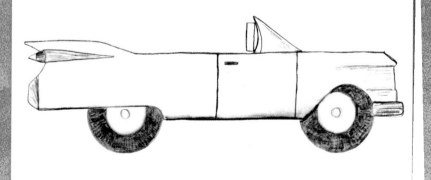

36 Ford Coupe Hot Rod

The Ford Coupe was designed in the mid to late 1930s. The Coupe makes an impressive street rod with its smooth lines. When flames are painted on the side of the Coupe, the car looks as if it is racing through a blaze of fire.

Step 1

Draw a thick rectangle. Draw a horizontal line across the rectangle. Draw a vertical line for the door.

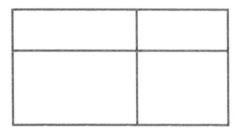

Step 2

Draw another vertical line for the door. Label the sections with the numbers one, two, and three. In sections one and three, draw circles for the back and front wheels.

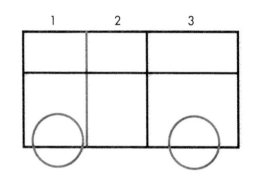

Step 3

Add two circles inside the wheels. Draw an arc for the roof.

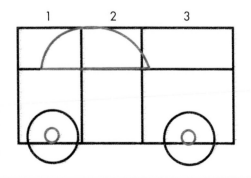

Step 4

In sections one and two, draw an arc for the windows. Draw two arcs above the tires.

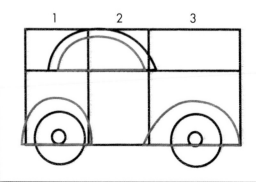

Step 5

In section one, draw a curved line for the trunk. In section two, draw an oval for the steering wheel. In section three, draw an oval for the grill and an oval for the headlight. Add a small curved line for the hood.

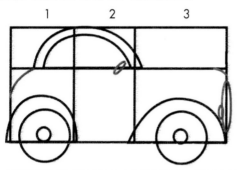

Step 6

Erase the rectangle, the numbers, and any other lines you no longer need. Trace over the shapes with a darker, sketchy line. Begin adding curved lines for flames. Begin shading in the tires.

Step 7

Add details. Draw a small rectangle for a door handle. Continue shading in the tires. Shade in the flames with the side of your pencil. Add two vertical lines inside the arc for the windows.

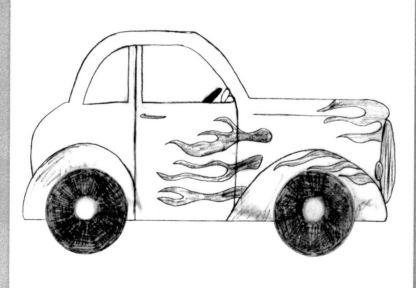

Police Car

Police cars are used to fight crime. A police car has a siren and flashing lights. When a driver sees the red, flashing lights of a police car, he or she needs to stop and let the police car pass.

Step 1

Draw a rectangle. Draw a horizontal line across the rectangle. Draw a vertical line down the center.

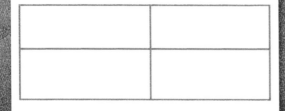

Step 2

Label the sections with the numbers one and two. In sections one and two, draw a trapezoid for the roof and two circles for the front and back wheels.

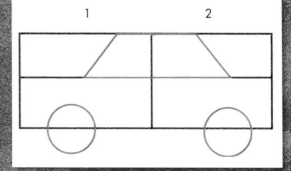

Step 3

In both sections, draw a trapezoid for the windows. In section one, draw a vertical line for the door. In section two, draw a zigzag line for the back door.

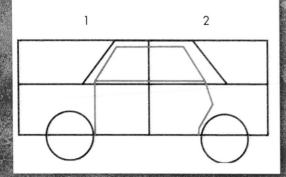

Step 4

Above section one, draw a small trapezoid for the light. In both sections, draw a long, slender rectangle for a painted stripe. Draw two circles in each wheel.

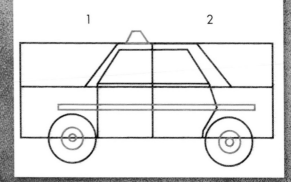

Step 5

In section one, draw an arc for the driver-side mirror. Draw an oval for the steering wheel. Add a slender rectangle for the front fender. In section two, add a small rectangle for the back fender.

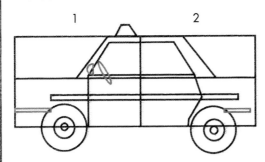

Step 6

Trace over the shapes with a darker, sketchy line. When tracing, curve the front hood and rear trunk. Add two vertical lines between the windows. Begin shading in the tires. Erase the lines you no longer need.

Step 7

Add details. Draw a rectangle for the front light. Add an arc for the rear light. Draw short rectangles for door handles. Write the word *POLICE* across the doors. Shade in the tires, the word *POLICE*, the light, and the rectangular stripes.

Volkswagen Beetle

The word Volkswagen means people's car. Ferdinand Porsche designed the first Beetle in the 1930s. The Beetle was affordable and easy to care for. Its body had a unique dome shape, like a beetle.

Step 1
Draw a large arc. Add a vertical line inside the arc.

Step 2
Label the sections with the numbers one and two. Draw two circles for the front and back wheels.

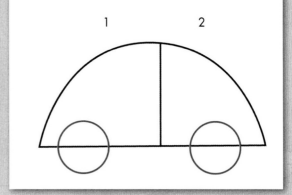

Step 3
In each section, draw an arc above the wheels. Draw an arc for the windows.

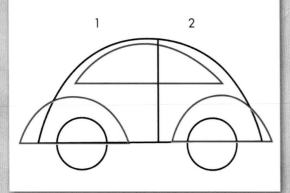

Step 4
Add two smaller circles inside each wheel. Draw two arcs for the front and back lights.

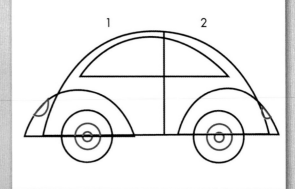

Step 5

In section one, draw a circle for the door handle. Separate the two windows with a rectangle. Draw an oval for the steering wheel. Add an arc for the mirror.

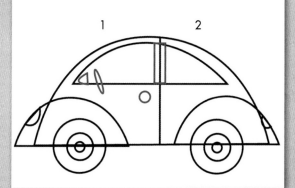

Step 6

Trace over the shapes with a darker, sketchy line. Add a curved line for the front hood. Connect the two fenders with a horizontal line. Begin shading in the tires. Erase the lines you no longer need.

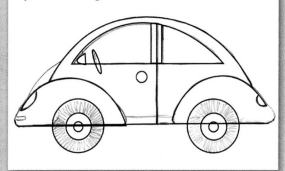

Step 7

Add details. Add a small rectangle for the door handle. Continue shading in the tires and steering wheel. Lightly shade the car, windows, and lights.

1995 McLaren F1 GTR

The GTR was built to race. The car made its debut at a famous race called the Le Mans, where it finished first overall. The GTR held four of the top five spots on its first day out.

Step 1
Draw a rectangle. Draw an arc above the rectangle.

Step 2
Draw a smaller arc inside of the arc to make the window. Draw a horizontal line across the bottom of the rectangle.

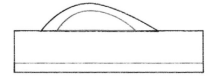

Step 3
Draw two circles for wheels. Draw a circle inside of the window for the helmet.

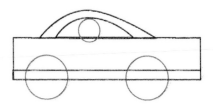

Step 4
Draw an upside-down triangle for the door. The triangle should meet the two edges of the window. Add two small circles in the front and back wheels.

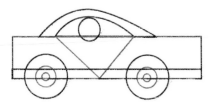

Step 5

Add a triangle in the front of the helmet for the driver to look through. Draw a vertical rectangle behind the driver's head. Draw an oval for the steering wheel.

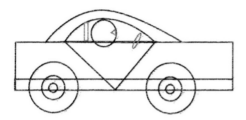

Step 6

Trace over the shapes with a darker, sketchy line. Draw a curved line for the front hood. Add a diagonal line for the back of the car. Add a curved line for the dashboard. Begin shading in the tires. Erase the lines you no longer need.

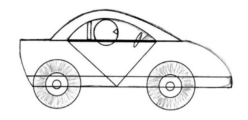

Step 7

Add details. Draw a curved line for the design on the side. Add diagonal stripes to the bar behind the driver's head and on the helmet. Shade in the curved line, tires, steering wheel, dashboard, and bumper.

Stretch Limousine

The stretch limousine is a luxury car that is driven by a chauffeur, or a special driver. A limousine can hold many passengers. A stretch limousine is built by adding a larger middle section to a regular-sized vehicle. The regular-sized vehicle is cut in half, and then another section of body is added in the middle.

Step 1
Draw a long, slender rectangle. Draw a horizontal line across the middle of the rectangle. Add two vertical lines for doors.

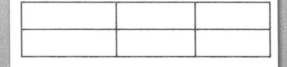

Step 2
Label the sections with the numbers one, two, and three. In section one, draw two circles for wheels. Add a diagonal line for the back window. In section three, draw one circle for the wheel. Draw a diagonal line for the window. In all three sections, draw a horizontal line.

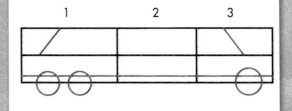

Step 3
In all three sections, draw two horizontal lines for the windows. Draw one at the top and one in the middle of the rectangle. Draw one small circle inside each of the wheels. In section one, draw a curved line for the back door.

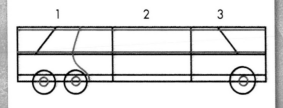

Step 4
In section two, draw two rectangles for windows. The rectangles should touch the horizontal lines. In section one, draw a rectangle for the rear light. In section three, draw a rectangle for the front light.

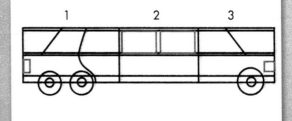

Step 5

In section three, draw a trapezoid for the front window. In section one, draw a trapezoid and heart for the back windows.

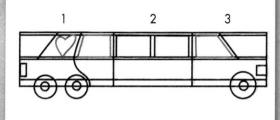

Step 6

Trace over the shapes with a darker, sketchy line. Begin shading in the tires and windows. Erase the lines you no longer need.

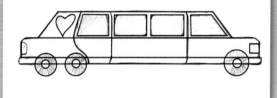

Step 7

Add details. Draw two rectangles for the door handles. Continue shading in the windows and tires.

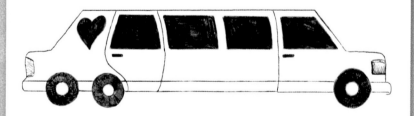

Land Rover

The Land Rover was first developed in 1948. It had four-wheel drive and could haul heavy loads. The Land Rover was perfect for the military and for use on farms.

Step 1
Draw a thick rectangle. Draw a horizontal line through the center of the rectangle. Add a vertical line.

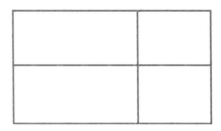

Step 2
Label the sections with the numbers one and two. In both sections, draw a horizontal line for the top of the windows. Draw two circles for the front and back wheels. Add a short vertical line for the door.

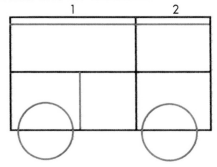

Step 3
Add two small circles in each wheel. In section one, draw a diagonal line for the front window. In section two, add a rectangle for the window.

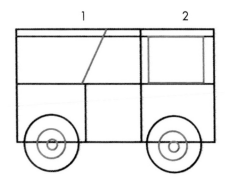

Step 4
In section one, draw a trapezoid window. Add a diagonal line for the hood. Add an oval for the spare tire.

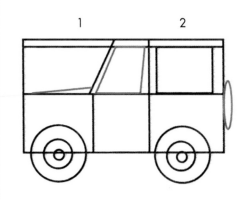

Step 5

In section one, draw an arc for the light and a rectangle for the bumper. Add an oval steering wheel. In section two, draw a rectangle bumper.

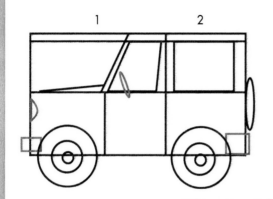

Step 6

Trace over the shapes with a darker, sketchy line. Draw a trapezoid shape around the top of the tires. Begin shading in the tires. Erase the lines you no longer need.

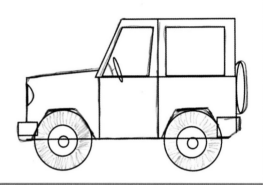

Step 7

Add details. Draw a small rectangle for the door handle. Continue shading in the tires, bumpers, and spare tire.

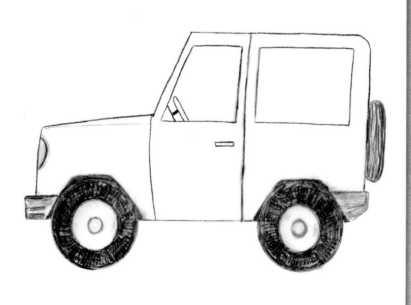

Nasty Beast

Like most monster trucks, Nasty Beast is a pickup body propped up on huge knobby tires. Nasty Beast rolls over smaller cars, crushing them as it bounces along to the roar of the crowd.

Step 1

Draw two squares and two rectangles for the body.

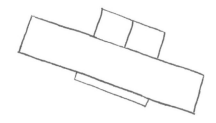

Step 2

Draw a square for the side window. Draw three diagonal lines for the front window. Add two arcs for the wheel wells.

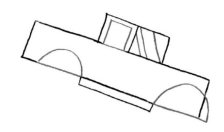

Step 3

Draw a rectangle for the back bumper and an arc for the front bumper.

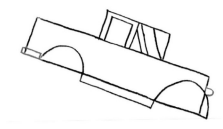

Step 4

Draw two more diagonal lines for the front window. Draw two circles for the tires. Add four circles for the hubcaps.

Step 5

Define the truck with a sketch line. Draw two curved lines for the door. Add a rectangle for the handle. Define the tires with wavy lines.

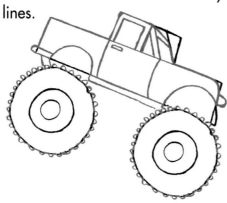

Step 6

Erase the extra lines. Add details such as zigzag lines for the teeth, an eye and arm with claws on the side, and an axle.

Step 7

Color your truck and add a background.

Colonel Crusher

Colonel Crusher has the body of a wood-paneled station wagon. But this is no family car! Its owner, a former U.S. Army colonel, gave the vehicle a very patriotic paint job.

Step 1

Draw a rectangle and a trapezoid for the body.

Step 2

Draw two arcs for the wheel wells. Draw a diagonal and vertical line for the windows.

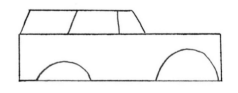

Step 3

Draw two circles for the tires. Add four circles for the hubcaps.

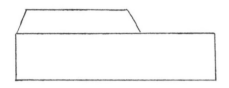
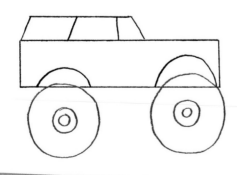

Step 4

Draw a large rectangle for the wood-paneled side. Add two rectangles for the bumpers.

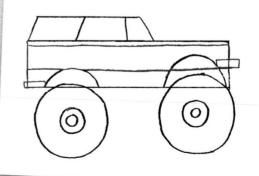

Step 5

Define the truck with a sketch line. Add a rectangle for the axle. Define the tires with wavy lines.

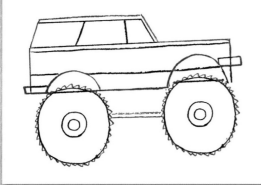

Step 6

Erase the extra lines. Add details such as stars, stripes, and an eagle on the side.

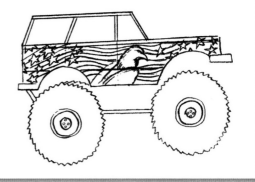

Step 7

Color your truck and add a background.

Tidal Wave

Tidal Wave has a sharp, racing look to it.
White and gold waves splash across its bright
blue hood and wash down the truck's sides.
Even the headlight covers are blue-tinted.

Step 1
Draw a trapezoid for the hood and a rectangle for the grill of the truck.

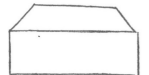

Step 2
Draw a horizontal line across the middle of the rectangle. Draw two trapezoids for the windshield.

Step 3
Draw four circles for the lights. Draw two rectangles for the tires.

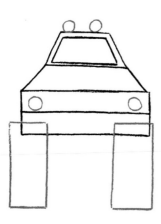

Step 4
Draw a rectangle and two diagonal lines for the axle.

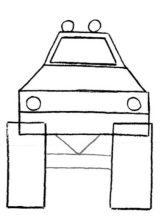

Step 5

Define the truck with a sketch line. Add a rectangle for the bumper. Define the tires with wavy lines.

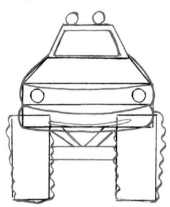

Step 6

Erase the extra lines. Add details such as tire treads, horizontal lines for the grill, and a wave on the hood.

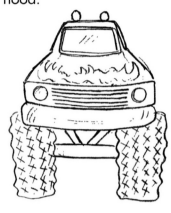

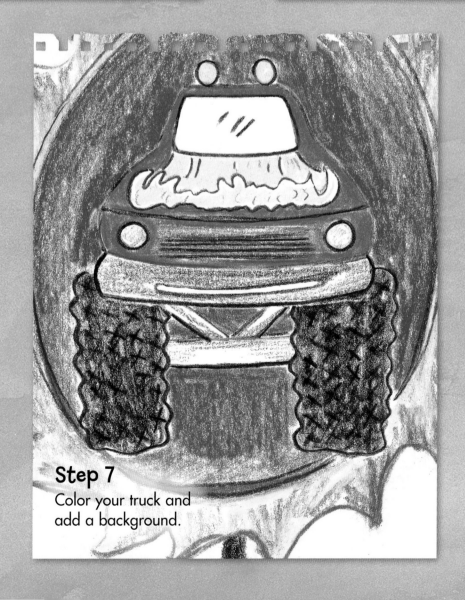

Step 7

Color your truck and add a background.

Rigormortis

Rigormortis is one of the most feared monster trucks of all. Its black paint job is highlighted with green flames. A graveyard scene, with ghosts and headstones, covers each side of this scary monster hearse.

Step 1
Draw two rectangles for the body.

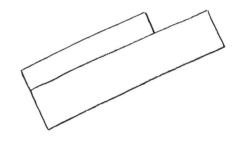

Step 2
Draw a diagonal line for the door. Draw two arcs for the wheel wells.

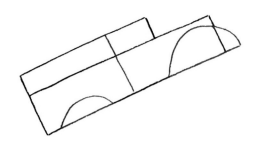

Step 3
Draw an oval for the headlight. Add one rectangle for the back bumper and another for the front bumper.

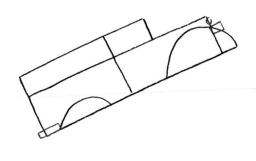

Step 4
Draw two circles for the tires. Add four circles for the hubcaps. Draw a rectangle for the window.

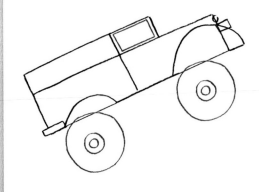

Step 5

Define the truck with a sketch line. Add two curved lines to shape the window. Define the tires with wavy lines.

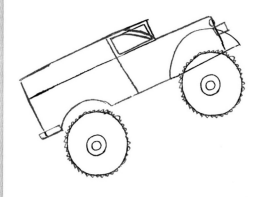

Step 6

Erase the extra lines. Draw a rectangle for the axle. Add details such as a ghost, headstones, and zigzag flames on the side.

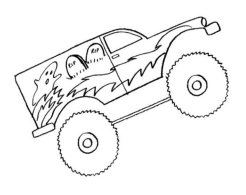

Step 7

Color your truck and add a background.

High Explosives

One of the most brightly colored monster trucks is High Explosives. It has white stars on a background of yellow, orange, red, and blue. The words "High Explosives" light up both sides.

Step 1
Draw two rectangles and two squares for the body.

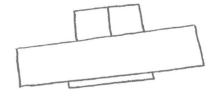

Step 2
Draw a square inside one square. Draw two diagonal lines inside the other square. Draw four arcs for the wheel wells.

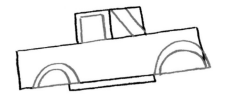

Step 3
Draw two diagonal lines for the window. Draw two circles for the tires. Add two circles for the hubcaps.

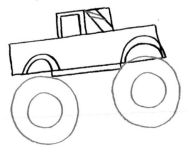

Step 4
Draw two arcs for the bumpers. Draw a rectangle for the axle. Add two stars to the hubcaps.

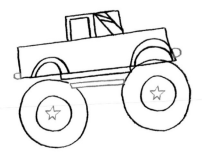

Step 5

Finish the side window with one diagonal line. Add two curved lines for the door. Define the truck with a sketch line. Define the tires with wavy lines.

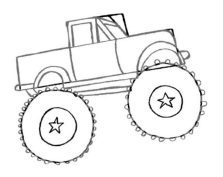

Step 6

Erase the extra lines. Add details such as dizzy lines, zigzag lines, and the words "High Explosives" on the side.

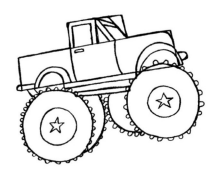

Step 7

Color your truck and add a background.

Bad Voodoo

Bad Voodoo sports crocodile teeth on its grill and sharp claws on its fenders. This monster sedan might just take a bite out of cars instead of crushing them!

Step 1

Draw three arcs for the front of the truck.

Step 2

Draw an arc for the roof and a trapezoid for the windshield.

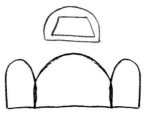

Step 3

Connect the roof to the front of the truck with two diagonal lines. Add two circles for the headlights.

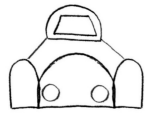

Step 4

Draw two rectangles for the tires. Add another rectangle for the axle.

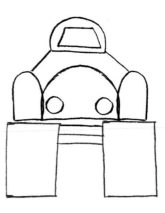

Step 5
Draw a rectangle for the bumper. Define the truck with a sketch line. Define the tires with wavy lines.

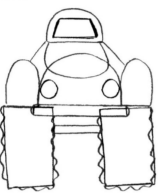

Step 6
Erase the extra lines. Add details such as tire treads, eyes, nostrils, and zigzag teeth and claws.

Step 7
Color your truck and add a background.

...ula

If you're afraid of spiders, this isn't the monster ...ou. Tarantula sports an all-black paint ...the rims are black. Across the sides ...d is a neon orange spider web.

Step 1

Draw three rectangles for the front and rear of the truck. Draw two circles for the headlights.

Step 2

Connect the front and back rectangles with four diagonal lines. You are creating a three-dimensional box. Draw two arcs for the wheel wells.

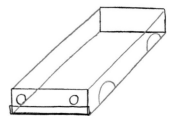

Step 3

Draw two rectangles for the windows. Draw three ovals and three curved lines for the tires. Add three ovals for the hubcaps.

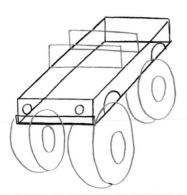

Step 4

Connect the front and back rectangles with two diagonal lines. Add a square for the side window and a rectangle for the windshield.

Step 5

Draw two diagonal lines for the door. Draw two horizontal lines for the axle. Define the truck with a sketch line. Define the tires with wavy lines.

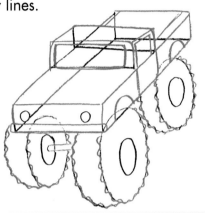

Step 6

Erase the extra lines. Add details such as a grill, a door handle, and a spider in a web on the hood.

Step 7

Color your truck and add a background.

Amy Bailey Muehlenhardt

Amy grew up in Fergus Falls, Minnesota, and attended Minnesota State University in Moorhead. She holds a Bachelor of Science degree in Graphic Design and Art Education. Before coming to Picture Window Books, Amy was an elementary art teacher. She always impressed upon her students that "everyone is an artist." Amy lives in Mankato, Minnesota, with her husband, Brad and two children, Elise and Jack.

Editors: Sara E. Hoffman and Kay M. Olson
Designers: Amy Bailey Muehlenhardt and Lori Bye
Art Director: Terri Foley
Production Specialist: Jane Klenk
The illustrations in this book were created with pencil and colored pencil.

Picture Window Books
1710 Roe Crest Drive
North Mankato, MN 56003
www.capstonepub.com

Printed in China
001821

Library of Congress Cataloging-in-Publication Data
Muehlenhardt, Amy Bailey, 1974-
  Beginner's guide to drawing / by Amy Bailey Muehlenhardt;
illustrated by Amy Bailey Muehlenhardt.
      p. cm. – (Sketch it!)
  ISBN 978-1-4048-6166-4 (pbk.)
  1. Drawing–Technique–Juvenile literature. I. Title.
  NC730.M74 2010
  741.2–dc22   2009045093